Pollyanna Age seven

This is the author's second experience at writing. Her first was an Autobiography describing her early life in Oklahoma during WWII and her subsequent move to California. She was married to a school administrator who died young. Following a successful career as a small business owner, she became a massage therapist and practiced for over twenty five years. She enjoyed writing her own story so much she decided to write a story about her great granddaughter who lives in Alaska because her life is so different than that of children who live in the lower forty eight.

ABOUT THE AUTHOR

This is the first published book of the Author. She wrote her own Autobiography, but chose not to publish it. She was a business owner for 25 years and later became a massage therapist.

LitPrime Solutions
21250 Hawthorne Blvd
Suite 500, Torrance, CA 90503
www.litprime.com
Phone: 1 (209) 788-3500

© 2021 Joyce Churchill. All rights reserved.

No part of this book may be reproduced, stored in a retrieval system, or transmitted by any means without the written permission of the author.

Published by LitPrime Solutions   02/11/2021

ISBN: 978-1-953397-76-8(sc)
ISBN: 978-1-953397-77-5(e)

Any people depicted in stock imagery provided by Thinkstock are models, and such images are being used for illustrative purposes only.

Certain stock imagery © Thinkstock.

Because of the dynamic nature of the Internet, any web addresses or links contained in this book may have changed since publication and may no longer be valid. The views expressed in this work are solely those of the author and do not necessarily reflect the views of the publisher, and the publisher hereby disclaims any responsibility for them.

ACKNOWLEDGEMENTS

I want to thank everyone who helped me tell my story. Grams, whose idea it was to write the book and helped compile my stories. Also, Mom, Grandmama and Grandpa Peter who were extremely helpful with their editorial input, including picture choice and other suggestions.

FOREWORD

Some adults think children should be seen and not heard. But I'm here to tell you that we kids have a lot to say. In fact, we have the best stories and adventures. I'm writing this book as if whomever is reading it is my BEST FRIEND. I may be only seven years old, but I've packed in a lot. I hope you enjoy learning about my life and my majestic home - - Alaska.

Happy Reading

PART ONE
ALASKAN ADVENTURES

CHAPTER ONE

MY STORY

XTRATUF boots "...part of what it means to be Alaskan."

My name is Polly, but my mom wrote "Pollyanna" on my birth certificate so people wouldn't know she named me after something she calls "The dead parrot sketch." I am not sure what that is all about, but she says I can watch it when I'm older. Pollyanna is okay with me though because I always have the longest name in my class, nine letters, and I learned it means humble or happy. I like that. My last name is Makabe, which is Japanese like my papa. Just to see me, I'm not much different than other seven-year-old girls.

Alaska is a unique place to grow up for sure, but we don't live in igloos or have polar bears as pets. Like many girls my age, I love cats and anything with flipping sequins. I sometimes fight with my mom about how much screen time I should be allowed on the weekend. I am not too tall or too short. Both my hair and my eyes are brown, and oh yeah, I have dimples.

Journaling, inspired by the great outdoors.

Having dimples is important for two reasons. See, my mom says I would not have lived to be seven years old if I did not have them. The other reason is because this was the first thing anyone ever knew about me. My mom did not want to know if I was going to be a boy or a girl before I was born. However, when I was born instead of saying "it's a girl" like you think she would, the nurse shouted out "look! Dimples!" None of that really matters though, because what you really need to know about me is that even though I was technically born in Nevada, I am an Alaskan girl. I have lived in Alaska most of my life, and I am "Alaska Tuff", just like my boots. If you aren't familiar, don't worry you will learn more about that later.

You might wonder why I want to write this book about myself. It started when Grams, who is my great grandmother, wrote a long autobiography when she was eighty-seven years old. I liked hearing about her life, especially the parts about when she was a kid just like me. Well, she grew up in Oklahoma so long ago there wasn't even televisions or Google, so maybe not *just* like me – but that is her story and this book is about me.

I got to thinking that maybe girls or boys might be interested in knowing how we live in Alaska, which is very different from living in the lower 48. When I visit down south even some adults seem to think I am an interesting child who has had many adventures. I'm hoping you will like to hear about them. Even better – I hope that after reading this story, you might want to try something like it on your own. Believe me, you will have loads of fun, and after all, our stories don't do us any good all locked up in our heads. Sharing them is the best way to learn about all the kinds of people in the world.

To understand my life in Alaska I have to explain some things about my family. There are lots of different kinds of families out there, and mine is one of the special ones. I live with my grandmama and my mom. Grandmama is a teacher and even though Mom also works in schools, she does lots of other things too. We have two small cabins in the forest. They are on a beautiful piece of land. When Grandmama bought it, there was only one small fishing cabin. And by cabin, I mean one room with no running water and no electricity. It did have a toilet in one of the closets, but without water or anywhere for the flushies to go, I honestly think whoever put it there missed the point of toilets.

We have been working on the cabins forever. In the beginning it was still pretty fun, kind of like camping. However, we didn't actually start out in Alaska roughing it. It took a lot of years for me to get that Alaska tough. When my mom and dad first brought me to Alaska, I was only 3 months old but I don't remember much about that time. But my mom loves to talk and I love hearing stories about bebe me and what a cute toddler I was.

Our Cabins. The "Castle" and the "Fort."

Here is a picture of a Moose in my frontyard.

CHAPTER TWO

A GIRL'S BEST FRIEND

BFF: Mr. Bear and Me

I have a pretty big family and even though Grandamama had already been living in Alaska for 8 years, a lot of the people down south were pretty sad to see me go when they were just getting to know me. Grams bought me a little white polar bear puppet in honor of my new Alaskan life. By the time she came for her first visit when I was 8 months old, I really loved that bear. He was soft and cuddly. He went everywhere with me—we were inseparable. If I misplaced him and couldn't find him, I made sure our house was chaos until he was found. As a bebe I was pretty good at letting people know when I was displeased.

One winter day, during my Gram's visit to Alaska, we went to the zoo. It was very cold, so my Mom put a warm jacket on me. I was born on the small side and it took me awhile to catch up so almost all my clothes were too big, like this coat. My family took me to see real polar bears that lived at the zoo. They thought I would be pretty excited about this and were saying, "Look, look. There is Mr. Bear". They were right, it was pretty exciting so I lifted my arm to point to the giant version of my best friend when disaster struck! My oversized sleeve had eaten up my hand. I looked down, and there at the end of my sleeve… nothing. Everyone said the look on my face was hilarious. The good news is that when I investigated, I found my hand down in that sneaky sleeve. Now you probably think I'm just re-telling what my family has told me. Of course everyone thinks their bebe is the cutest and does the funniest things and it probably wasn't even all that great in real life. Lucky for me, Peter, my great grandfather, always had a video camera in his hand. I've seen the whole thing and I'm here to tell you, it was hilarious.

Sadly, about two years later, Mom lost Mr. Bear on a trip to the store. It was just before Thanksgiving and that year we had a big trip to the top of the world to celebrate in Wainwright, Alaska. By the time we got back he was gone even though we went back to the store to ask if he had been found. My Grams did buy me another one, but it just wasn't the same.

My hand! Whew, there it is after all

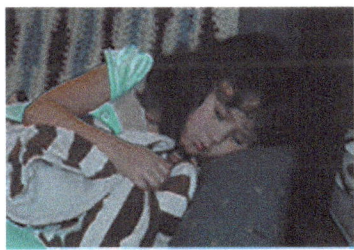

Even my cats, Tiger and Lili, like my monkey blanket

Mom felt so bad she got me a new cuddly, which brings me to another important thing in my life. My blanket. Also known as monkey or just monk. Yes, I'm seven . . . don't judge me. I'm sure you have a "blankie" or fuzzy toy or animal that is special to you, so you know what I'm talkin' about. My Monk is brown and white and has three cute sock monkey heads on one corner. I must have it to sleep and cuddle because it is part of me. The best part is that after Mr. Bear, Mom was SO freaked out she bought a couple of *emergency* blankets—I think I'm up to four. I can always find one. She says that when I get big enough she will even sew them all together to make one gigantic Monk.

CHAPTER THREE

THE LAY OF THE LAND

I need to take a little step back. I told you about how Mr. Bear got lost right before our trip to Wainwright. You are probably thinking, what the heck? Where in the world is that? Alaska is a big place. I mean a really big place. My cousins live in Texas now, and I've learned down there they say everything is bigger in Texas. I got news for all you Texans – the entire state of Texas, would fit inside Alaska. Alaska is by far the BIGGEST state of them all. Now a lot of Alaska is uninhabitable – that means nobody can live there, but that isn't the point. In fact one of the greatest things about Alaska is that even though we have the most space we have almost the smallest population. That is why it is so beautiful here. Lots of uninterrupted nature.

When we first moved to Alaska, we lived in a little town about an hour outside of Anchorage called Wasilla. This is known as south-central Alaska. Wasilla is probably most famous for being the hometown of Sarah Palin, a former Governor of Alaska. I don't know much about politics and I never met her, but I remember her house. We passed by it almost every day

Continental U.S. 1,868,591 sq. mi., Alaska 566,432 sq. mi., Texas 262,970 sq. mi.

and mom would always point it out and say, "Hey, bebe, it just goes to show you, no matter how far you go you can't get away from home." That's because Mrs. Palin lives on Nevada Street and that is where mom grew up and where I was born.

So, when I was two years old, Grandmama decided she really missed living and teaching in bush Alaska. The bush is what they call the villages that are off the road system and are so remote you can only get there by plane, or sometimes boat. This is how I ended up going to the Alaskan Native village, Wainwright, for Thanksgiving. Wainwright is not in South central Alaska. It is way way way up North above the Arctic Circle, called "The Slope" by us Alaskans. Even if you don't live in a village, bush planes are a big part of Alaskan life. The thing you need to know about bush planes is that they are small. So small they don't even have heaters, let alone things like flight attendants that bring you apple juice. When I visited Wainwright and flew on my first bush plane I had to wear full snowgear, and still my nose froze. I was not amused. The nice thing about bush planes is that they fly pretty low so you can get some great views. Of course this wasn't the case in November, because even though it was almost lunch time, it was still dark. Most people ask what it is like to have so much darkness. It is true that we have very little light in the winter, but it's really not so bad. It is also true that up on the Slope there is a time when they have full days of darkness but down in south central we get daylight around ten am, and then it starts getting dark again around four pm. The hardest part of this is going to school and playing on the playground before school in complete darkness. The only light comes from the school windows. Add a playground covered with ice and temperatures of ten below (less than 10 below is when we can have indoor recess) and you would think Alaskan kids have it pretty tough. But, that's just how we get our name 'cause it doesn't even slow us down.

Going "over water" in the air taxi

Summer does make up for all that darkness of winter. We have very little darkness in the summer. In Summer, I can play outside until after Midnight because it's so bright and beautiful you just can't sleep! Mom does make me go to bed eventually, of course. We have black-out curtains and I use an eye mask to help me feel sleepy.

When I was about to turn three, I was just getting old enough to really be doing some learning about the world,

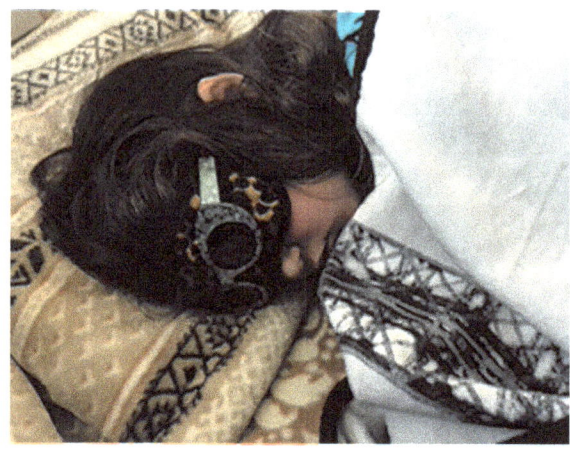

Sleeping with eye mask AND sunglasses in the land of the midnight sun.

and forming my first memories. Except that, I was so little I couldn't quite remember the winter before, only the summer. When I got up the sun was up and shining, when I went to bed, still there. I hadn't seen the dark in months. Then fall came and the day came for me to start preschool. The days were finally getting shorter, and all of a sudden I had to get up earlier to get to school. I didn't trust that darkness at first because I didn't remember it AT ALL. I only knew daylight so when my mom would open up the door, I would grab on to her neck tightly and bury my face in her chest until we got to the car. I'm not afraid of the dark anymore though, because I know our long long nights are just part of being Alaskan tough.

CHAPTER FOUR

SMARTY PANTS

Sometimes even princesses need to get their hands dirty. Baking a cake.

The preschool I went to was a Montessori school. This was a good opportunity for me because they teach a lot of things that regular pre-schools don't teach. Like how to be independent and do things for ourselves. Cool things like cooking, and not so fun things like cleaning up after. Even though it's not my favorite part, I do it because I know you have to be responsible. I also learned things like math by adding with the stamp game and writing by tracing all my letters in sand while making their sounds.

I have always loved books and reading, even before preschool. My dad even read to me when I was still in Mom's tummy. Maybe that is why I love books. I have a ton of them. When I was a tiny baby one of the first pictures of me was being all swaddled up and lying on a bed, rockin' the burrito look and staring at a book. As soon as I learned to walk, I started carrying anything with words to my mom. Once she even read a video game system owner's manual to me for almost 15 minutes. She got bored before I did.

Sometimes my mom would try to skip sentences or even pages in my picture books, but I always caught her. I figured out how to read on my own when I was almost four, but did not even let anyone know it for a while. Sometimes they asked if I could read a word they pointed to on the page and that was okay, but it would interrupt the story. I would have to remind my reader to go back. I love the way they use their voices to make the stories come to life. When they wanted me to read something, I always said, "Now, you read it with expression". That is because I didn't really want people to find out how much I could read. I liked hearing the different voices and watching Mom's face as she read to me and I was worried if they knew I could do it myself our story times would be over.

Even on Christmas morning, with all the new toys IN THE WORLD – my favorite thing to do is read

Then the day came when they finally caught me. My grandmama was fussing because somebody moved the bookmark in her book, <u>Bad Girls of the Bible</u>. She was arguing with my 25-year-old cousin, who she thought must have been the culprit. I finally said, "I'm reading that book." You can imagine how much everybody laughed at that! I got really mad when nobody believed me. So, I got the book, opened to a page, and read it. The names were a little crazy so I had to just make them up or skip over, but I could read most of the rest of it. They weren't laughing then. I think they were just too surprised because everyone's eyes got pretty wide.

Now that I am seven everyone knows I can read, but Grandmama or Mom still read to me at bedtime. I am really fascinated by words and have always wanted to know about big and unusual words. When I come across a word that I don't know I ask, or now that I am old enough to Google it on my iPad. All those words from reading get into my brain and now they just pop out when I need to use them. People are always laughing about the way I talk. What? I love fancy words.

On my third Halloween, I was getting ready in my Snow White Costume. My mom was telling the story of how Snow White got her name and her beauty after the queen accidently pricked her finger and saw a drop of her blood on the snow. This inspired her to wish for a daughter with white skin and red lips. I really wanted to wear make-up as part of my costume and so I told Mom that the story was "preposterous" and that I clearly needed some lipstick. She thought it was so funny I knew that word, and could use it correctly that I even got my way.

A delicious apple. Go ahead and try one.

CHAPTER FIVE

THERE ARE A LOT OF FISH IN THE SEA... AND THE RIVER... AND THE LAKE

Alaska is known for its glaciers and beautiful scenery. It is also known for its salmon fishing. There is no better place for this than the Kenai Peninsula. Just before my third birthday we moved from Wasilla to Soldotna. This area is also known as Alaska's playground because of all the visitors we get in the summer. Alaskans and people from all over the world come to fish, hunt, hike, and play outdoors. Salmon aren't the only fish we have, but they are special.

There are five types of salmon. In Alaska we have a good trick to keep them straight. You can do this as you read along to remember too. First, hold out your thumb. This is for the chum salmon, because it rhymes. Next is the pointer finger, be careful you don't poke out your eye – like the sockeye salmon. King salmon are the most famous, because they are bigger than the rest, just like your middle finger. Silvers, sure are pretty – shiny like jewelry on your ring finger. The last is the pinks. You guessed it, the pinky finger represents those fish.

Unlike most fish, salmon live in both the ocean and freshwater. They start off life in rivers, then when they are strong enough they swim out to sea. Depending on the species, they grow bigger for three to five years, until it is time to lay eggs of their own. This is called spawning. When it is time to spawn they swim all the way back up the rivers to where they hatched. Amazing right? The salmon get ready to lay eggs all at the same time during the year. When this happens, there are lots and lots of salmon, which makes them easier to catch.

Grandmama and my cousin Roxy with some of our catch.

There are also lots and lots of fishers. Along the banks of the river they stand shoulder to shoulder in some places. We call this combat fishing. As any doctor in town can tell you it can be dangerous too. There are a lot of emergency room visits to remove fish hooks during the fishing season. If you are a tourist, you have to fish using a fishing pole. However, if you are an Alaskan resident, you are allowed to go dip netting. It is just like it sounds, you dip your net in the water, and scoop up the fish. Some people do this from a boat, floating down the river. My family usually does it from the shore though. It is easier to catch fish this way because on their way to spawn they aren't very hungry so it can be hard to get them to go after bait.

The reason Alaskans are allowed to fish this way is that many Alaskans don't work in they same way people down south do. They either don't have a traditional job, or they only work part of the year, and only part time. The rest of the time they use their time for subsistence. This means they hunt and fish and pick berries or gather other food to feed their families. Even though Alaska is part of the United States, it's cut off and it is very expensive to get things from the rest of the country. Filling up our freezers with salmon every summer is very important. Only Alaskans are allowed to dipnet because it is also really important to protect the salmon by not catching too many each year.

"Kangaroo" dipnetting with Grandmama

While it is easier to get those fish in the net than on a hook, dipnetting isn't easy. The water is really cold and it is hard work. From the beach you have to stand in the water where the ocean and the river meet, fighting the waves from the ocean and the current from the river. There are a ton of people and everyone wants to keep a good spot to put their net in. You stand there for hours bringing enough fish for the whole year. My grandmama does that part of it. My mom is on the beach doing the cleaning of the fish and getting them ready for the freezer. Some people just gut their fish and do the rest at home. You have to be careful at home because the smell from the fish waste can attract bears. That is why my family likes to cut up our fish at the beach.

I haul water from the ocean to mom because she needs a lot of it to clean all those salmon. Sometimes I hit the fish on the head with the club, or even a stick. A lot of really little kids go out with their nets, and Grandmama says soon I will too. For now, I'd rather stay on beach crew. I get to play in the sand and the water. My mom has this really cool trick, because the fish are so fresh. When she guts the salmon, she sometimes sets the heart on the cutting table all by itself. Then, if she pokes at is just right it keeps beating! It's a little gross, I guess, pumping away, but it just goes to show you – in Alaska even the fish are extra tough.

Some of the Alaskans that dipnet are from Anchorage, or even farther away. Even though we live nearby the river, we still camp on the beach for about a week because it is easier than packing our gear in and out everyday. I like the middle of the week because it isn't so crowded, but there aren't as many other kids to play with. On the weekend there is also a Christian mission group that always comes to the beach to give all the fishermen free hot dogs and drinks. They have many activities including a bounce house right on the beach. Even though I don't really know most of the people, it is like one big party. My family makes campfires on the beach for s'mores.

Setting up fish camp

Alaskans are usually really nice because we are used to all working together. Even though we might not really know each other, during dipnetting season, I kind of feel like we are one big Alaskan family.

Dipnetting during a run.
The beach at Kenai during dipnetting season

CHAPTER SIX

PASSIONS

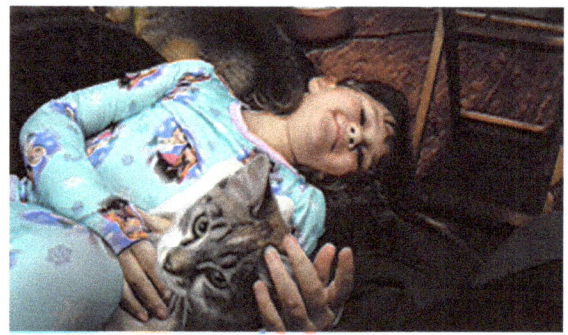
Loving Lili

There are two things in this world this Alaskan Snow Princess, as my Oma calls me, can't live without. The first is kittens. Cats are okay too, but you can't beat a kitten. They are so small and fluffy and kitten-like. This is one of those things that make me, me. Most of my family are "dog people." Dogs are okay… kinda. We have one too. His name is Moka and he is great at keeping us safe from bears and moose. Especially the bears, because they smell him and don't want to come around the house. The moose kind of just stand there chewing in a bored way while he barks at them, but at least we know when they are in the driveway or out behind the house and we can be extra careful. This part of my story isn't about Moka though, it's about cats.

As I said, I LOVE KITTENS AND CATS! I was just a baby but I've been told this story a million times. My family was fostering a cat named Buddy. This was before I was old enough to talk, and so I hadn't convinced Momma to get me my very own forever cat yet. Buddy loved me like I was his own kitten. He was a big guy, bigger than me even though I was almost a year old, and he loved to sleep in my crib. When anyone came to take the cat out of the crib, the cat would attack and hiss because he was protecting me. The cat never left my side, even when I pulled his tail and whiskers. Cats don't usually like babies so Momma started calling me "*Cat Whisperer.*" All cats just love me to death.

Now, I have two grown cats named Tiger and Lily. I am beginning to think, that I really am a cat, because I have everything on or about cats in every part of my life. As I'm writing this, it is getting close to Halloween. I'm getting my costume ready and I'll bet you can guess what it is going to be. You are right -- a cat. I have kitten and cat pictures on my dresses, hats, gloves, house shoes, reading books, coloring books, and so forth. I even go around mewing a lot.

One of my Play Doh crafts

I have perfected a "cat dance". I put on cat pajamas and my favorite set of cat ears. Next I get in my "cat pose," which I learned during yoga at my preschool. One of the adults puts on a good song like, "Can't Stop the Feeling." As soon as the music starts, the cat part of me takes over and does an amazing dance. Once Grams taped it and when I watched it after I thought, "Is that me or a real cat?" I also like to draw all kinds of kittens, and if I'm making something, you can guess it's a cat.

Buddy, my cuddle buddy and protector

That brings me to my next passion. Creating things, especially tiny things for all my stuffies, tiny friends, and baby pets. The baby pets are mostly imaginary, but the stuffies and tiny toys are real. My mother calls me a hoarder. That's because I like to make things from "throw-away" items, or from any odd items I find around my house. If you open up something and there is a piece of cardboard you are going to throw away, I already have an idea of what I can make. My favorites are foam cushioning, any kind of clear plastic, and fabrics.

"Shark Tank" is one of my favorite television shows, and I decided I should invent something to get me on their program. If you have never heard of Shark Tank, it is a show on TV where people show their inventions to possible investors. I got an idea for a toy that was both a stuffy, a tiny friend, and would teach kids their shapes. It was made from two triangles out of felt. After sewing them together I stuffed it. A happy cat face drawn on one side and a sad cat face on the other side completed my invention. I can think of many ways that a child would have fun playing with these. I also made a "happy face/sad face" puppy circle. There could have been other animals made from shapes, but after much thought, I decided I would not be able to keep up with production, if they liked it. They ask kids a lot how they are going to finish their education and run a business. Education is also important to my family so I don't think I would be allowed to become a business person so young. Oh well - - I'll think of something else, when I get a little older.

No, this isn't halloween, just me in my cat gear on a regular day.

I love "Bad Kitty" books, by Nick Bruel. I know, big surprise. I drew this picture from instructions in one of the books while on vacation in Mexcio

I have made some other very unusual items. For instance, when I was about four and a half, I needed a doll house for my Calico Critters. So, I used cardboard I found, and with the help of duct tape, I made a two story doll house. I even made some cardboard furniture and colored the pieces. My critters and I loved it. It's amazing what can be done with cardboard and duct tape.

Another time, I decided I needed a wallet. I found some pink felt and used it to cut out two rectangles, which I sewed together. I left a flap and sewed a buttonhole to close it with. It's really neat. Sometimes, I amaze myself. I picture things in my mind and then just go ahead and make them. You could do the same things I do. Just use your imagination. You will be surprised at the results. Plus, if you have a well thought out plan it is a lot easier to talk your mom into letting you keep "trash," even if she thinks you are a hoarder.

CHAPTER SEVEN

HOME IS WHERE YOUR PLANE LANDS

I have a confession. Yes, I am an Alaskan Tough girl. Yes, I love an adventure, the outdoors, animals, and playing under the midnight sun. As it turns out I also love long baths, even though I'm secretly a cat, I have my own room (decorated with cats), and a thermostat. This year we have moved to a small fly-in village outside of Homer on English Bay. There are some things that are more challenging, but since Grandmama is a teacher and Momma works for the school too we get to live in teacher housing.

Our NO water closet

We still have our little place across the water in Kasilof. You remember the one? In the beginning, there was no running water, no indoor toilet and no heat. Now, we have all of those in Grandmama's house, but my cabin is still a one room cabin without running water or a real heater. You should appreciate your bathrooms and running water. Without them, some people think life is a pain, but remember, I'm an Alaska girl. It's not that unusual to live in dry cabins in Alaska. The summer is no big deal and I even like going to the bathroom out in nature when I use the "honey bucket." Sometimes I even go out of Grandmama's house, where the toilet is, just to use the bucket. There aren't any neighbors that can see so I leave the tent flap open and enjoy the view while I use the "facilities."

I also like that we can change the houses and the property how we like. Momma had a great idea to add a small loft to our cabin so I could have my own space. Grandmama did a great job designing it and I love laying up there. The only problem is that it still doesn't have it's own way up so I use a ladder, and sometimes they take my ladder for other projects so I can't use my loft for a few days until they give it back.

The permafrost in Alaska makes the soil bad, so we have to bring in better stuff.

Seeding my lawn with Tiger.

Playing outside could get kind of dirty, which is a problem when you don't have running water, so I asked Grandmama if I could have a lawn. As usual she said "If you want one, I'll teach you to plant one". It wasn't easy. I had to fill the wheelbarrow with dirt and spread it out. And then again and again. I planted the seeds with a seed spreader and watered them. It was exciting to watch the little blades of grass grow. Now, I have a nice lawn to play on.

Another time, I decided I wanted a rock garden, which eventually turned into a large fairy garden. I think I got the idea because my Grams has two fairy gardens and my Great Uncle also has one. So, you guessed it, I got out the wheelbarrow and made a fairy garden. My cousin, Noah, (who is twelve and was visiting from Nevada), helped me arrange all the tiny people and houses in the garden. We both built and decorated some of the houses before placing them along the paths we made. It's fun to keep adding to all the different sections with those tiny things I love to build.

I found and gathered each and every rock for the perimeter of fairy garden island myself.

We call this "reception" rock, because it's the only place in Nanwalek we've found a cell signal

Now I have the best of both worlds because we will still spend most of the summer in Kasilof, but in the winter we are in Nanwalek. More about the village life. First, Nanwalek is so beautiful. We can see the ocean from our living room. I feel like we are living on an island because our little village is tucked right up against a mountain so there is no place to go beyond the village. Also, since our house was built on school property, my backyard is an entire playground, two actually. We are up on a hill and once it snows this is also the best sledding hill in the village.

Like I said, Nanwalek is very small. It is only 8.4 square miles, where we live and play is even smaller than that. There are a few cars but most people just walk. Some have quads or small utility vehicles. We do have two stores. There is one church and a community center. This is nice because it makes it a safe place. I am even allowed to go shopping on my own, if I ask my mom first. The store by the school has a Slushie machine, which is currently my favorite treat.

Most everyone here, besides my family and some of the other teachers, were born here like their parents, and their grandparents, and back and back and back. They are the Sugpiaq people and I even get to learn the Sugt'stun language as part of my school day. It is very challenging, but I understand a little more everyday, even if speaking it is coming slowly. My Sugpiaq name is Kuskaq, which means cat. I know, right? The kids here grow up eating traditional foods like Akuutaq, a dessert made with seal oil and berries. Although, around here they usually make it with Crisco, potatoes, and berries. The recipe changed because seal hunting isn't as common as it once was in this part of Alaska. One of the favorite snacks served at my school is palik, dried salmon. Other subsistence foods most families harvest in Nanwalek include amikuq (octopus) that is used to make a really good dish with rice, and caqallqaq (seaweed) which is used for all kinds of things.

There are lots of traditions in the village, but they actually come from two cultures. Before Alaska became part of the United States, Russians explored and settled in a lot of the area. There are even villages that call themselves "old believers" where they still speak Russian as their main language, wear clothing of old world Russia and keep other Russian customs. Here in Nanwalek the Russian traditions mix with the Sugpiaq culture. The church is Russian Orthodox and they have their own calendar, so our winter break is in January for Russian Christmas, instead of December following the English calendar.

Even though it is a close community, I have made lots of friends in the short time I have been here. Starting the third grade was exciting. There are 17 kids in my class, but we also have 4th and 5th graders in with us third grade students. Best of all I met a girl who loves cats almost as much as I do!

CHAPTER EIGHT

ALASKAN CUSTOMS

Traveling has its perks, but as Momma says, we live in Alaska for a reason. We like it! People have some funny ideas about Alaska. Some of these ideas come from TV shows like "Deadliest Catch." The Time Bandit, one of the fishing boats from the show, docks out of Homer which is where we catch the air taxi in and out of Nanwalek. However, other shows like "Life Below Zero," and "Alaska State Troopers" are about different parts of Alaska and aren't really like my life at all.

Other ideas people in the lower 48 have about Alaska are just plain crazy pants. We do not live in igloos. We do not have penguins. When Momma announced we were moving to Alaska when I was just three months old, four people bought me a snowsuit. Yes, we have snow, but we also have houses and wear regular clothes most of the day. In fact since we have been here my Uncle in Lake Tahoe has had more snow most years than me – and that is in California!

We do have some fun winter activities though, like fishing in the winter on frozen lakes. One of the annual field trips I got to go on in first and second grade is ice fishing. Fish and game does a great job helping all the kids out on the ice. They make sure the ice is thick enough to be safe. Then they take something called an ice auger, which is a giant metal spiral with handle to crank it around, and make holes to put our lines down in the water. The ice chunks will float around in the hole and clog it up so we use wire scoops to clean them out. They also set up shelters for when we need to take a break. There is a competition every year for the kid that catches the biggest fish. At the assembly to celebrate the end of the ice fishing derby the kids get to vote on a teacher who has to kiss

L'Amour et l'Amitié

a fish! It's so funny, because I'm not the one that has to kiss a slimy fish. I actually caught my very first fish out on the ice. It was a trout, and Grandmama's friend, who was helping me learn, taught me how to clean it right. Momma cooked it up and we had it for dinner. I liked it so much better than salmon, but that might just be because I caught it myself.

Even though it is cold in the winter months, when we are out having fun fishing, playing in the snow, or riding around on snow-gos (that's a snowmobile for those of you down south) we still have to be careful about the sun. The snow is so white, for so far, it reflects the sun back at us. If you aren't careful you can get sunburn from both the sun and the reflection. It also makes it very bright and you can go snow blind if you don't protect your eyes. We learn to dress in layers because mucking through the snow can be hard work and if you bundle up too much you can overheat, but if you don't bundle enough you can also get frostbite. It can be kind of confusing having to worry about the sun and overheating and the cold of the snow at the same time.

CHAPTER NINE

XTRATUF - AN AFTERWORD

I can't believe I almost forgot! In the beginning I promised I would explain XTRAtufs, and yet here we are. You read all the way to the end of my story and not a word about this strange thing - the XTRAtuf. An XTRAtuf is a type of boot. It looks a little like a rain boot. They are dark brown on the outside with a tan border near the sole. Their logo is red, and they all look somewhat similar. Everyone, and I mean EVERYONE in Alaska has, and loves their XTRAtufs. They really represent your classic Alaskan. If you aren't paying attention, they look like any old rain boot, but really, they are so much more. They are thicker and, ah hem, tougher than your average boot. Even though they have similar characteristics, they also have unique differences. Some are shorties, some go up to the knee, some are plain, some have fancy designs on the inside. They come in all sizes, and are worn in different ways by their owners. Like Alaskans they are durable, easily recognizable, but in their own way each pair possess their own character.

My XTRAtufs have gotten me through seven seasons of mucky, muddy break-up. Seven summers of fishing on the beach. Seven rainy Falls of puddle jumping. Not going to lie, they aren't real useful in the winter, not warm enough so they go up on the shelf while the snow boots do their work. I'm on my fourth pair of XTRAtufs, because my feet keep growing along with the rest of me. I am always a little sad when it is time to pass on my too small XTRAtufs, with their memories, to exchange for new ones. Though, I do like knowing, they will be there, to get me through my next Alaskan adventure.

We see a lot of Northern Lights like this

PART TWO
OTHER FUN TIMES

CHAPTER TEN
WORLD TRAVELER

Alaska is an exciting place all year round, but even living here sometimes a girl needs a break. I am lucky, because I get to see my down-south family once or twice a year and we go to some pretty cool places together. Most of the time we meet in Northern Nevada or Northern California, but sometimes we go traveling together. I'm only seven, but I've already been to eight states, and Mexico.

I have a lot of Aunties. My mom doesn't have any sisters, but her and Grandmama have some really great friends we call my Aunties. This comes from a tradition in the village where all adult, respected, women are referred to as Aunties, even if they are not blood related. One of my favorites is Auntie Pam. We have a tradition where we always spend 4th of July together, even when I was just a baby! A couple of times we got to celebrate at family camp in South Lake Tahoe, California. In addition to my Auntie Pam, there was my Mom, Grandmama, Grams, Grandpa Peter my Aunt Stacy and Uncle Travis and their son Noah, who is my older cousin, and another family friend, Auntie Jane. We all had a great time, together.

Auntie Pam at Family Camp

Whew! It was a family houseful. Since there were so many of us, we got to stay in a two story house at the camp. It had lots of space and had a very large table in the main room where we played board games at night, after a short campfire. Since it's camp I get to stay up extra late to play games. Yippie! Oh, there were so many things to do. Some of the fun things we do are swimming and kayaking in beautiful Lake Tahoe, which I did a lot. The water is very cold and the adults sometimes think kids like me, jumping in and out of the water from the giant water trampoline, are crazy. No matter how cold, you can't keep me out of the water.

We also did lots of crafts, such as tye-dye T shirts, and making many fruit pizzas in a Tandoori oven. Also, all kinds of nature crafts. At the end of the week, there is a talent show. Our family wrote a skit about a bear. It was really funny. Grandpa Peter made a puppet out of an oven mitt and did a ventriloquist act. Everyone loved it and he got lots of applause. I think every child should have at least one camp experience. You get to meet lots of people and make new friends, learn a lot of new things, eat good food, experience nature and the outdoors. I LOVE IT.

Another tradition my family enjoys is spending a few weeks in Nuevo Vallarta, Mexico. Grams and Grandpa Peter go every year, and I have been there twice. The first time I was five and then again last year, when I was seven. Grams and Grandpa Peter go to a beautiful resort there with lots of palm trees and a great beach. It's like a tropical jungle. Sometimes there are iguanas or amazing birds to see just walking along to the pools. And those pools! There are lots of pools to swim in. Big pools, little pools. Pools of all different shapes, one with a lazy river to float along. One even has a place right in the middle of the water where you can go order a juice. You can have it right in a pineapple made to look like a monkey. While you sip on your juice you can sit on a little stool next to the counter and enjoy the sun without ever even leaving the pool. Until my mom makes me take a sunscreen break that is. There is even a small pool on the balcony of the apartment, so basically I swim all day long.

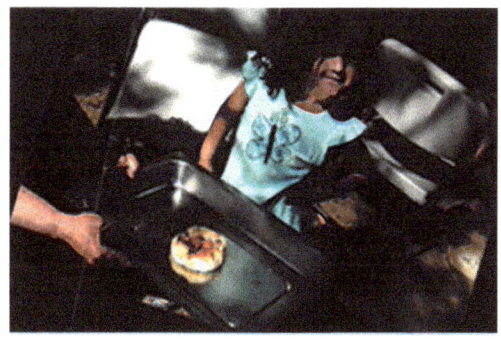

Fruit pizza made in a Tandoori oven

Painting a ceramic…you guessed it, cat.

I do get dragged away from the pools sometimes. I got to do a neat craft, there. I hand painted a small pottery cat bank, which was later heated to a glaze. It is very pretty. The second year I painted a turtle. It is fun but you really have to concentrate. I also painted an apron, which I enjoy wearing. Another amazing thing I did in Mexico was to visit a chocolate factory. The chocolate begins with a small pod, and goes through several processes before it becomes the chocolate that we know. They gave us (my family with me) chef's hats and aprons, and then we got to make our own chocolate candies. We poured the liquid chocolate into molds. We got to choose the shape we wanted from several types. We made twelve pieces of candy, which then were put into a freezer to cool and solidify. While we were waiting, we went upstairs to have a snack and dessert. We got to take our pretty chocolates home in a fancy box. It was delightful.

Each night the hotel had a show. The show I liked the most, which was not on the resort, however is called "Rhythms of the Night". We went on a boat ride to the show, had dinner, and then the show, which was dancing and drumming by Mayan people. On the return boat trip, the crew entertained us with funny acts. I loved everything about that night. The deskman at the hotel told Grandmama that the show might be too long or scary for someone as little as me. He was wrong, wrong, wrong. The dancers were everywhere, even flying in from the sky. The costumes were like nothing I had ever seen before, it made all the actors look like real animals.

My day as a chocolatier.

I didn't think anything would top Rhythms of the Night, but on the next trip I got to go swimming with the dolphins. I got to pet them and even had a chance to give one of them a kiss. Then, I got to hold onto the tail of a dolphin and be pulled around the pool, for a ride. Very exciting. If you ever get a chance to swim with dolphins, do it - - it's lots of fun. I still love dancing shows, but spending time with a real live dolphin is a different kind of fun. Having all kinds of experiences is a big part of my life. This is one reason I am such a good Alaskan.

Dancers from the nightly show at our resort.

CHAPTER ELEVEN

COUSINS

It is great to have new best friends, but you can never have too many awesome people in your life. Even though we only see each other a couple times a year I LOVE hanging out with my cousins. I have two adult cousins, but I also have two cousins that are pretty close to my age and we have so much fun together. During most of the year we keep in touch through the internet with Messenger and Facetime and things like that. When we get together one of our favorite things to do is entertain our family.

We are a talented bunch. Noah plays the violin. Anna, the oldest, is also musical but she plays the piano. Her sister, Mae is a great artist and they both play a lot of sports. Fiona and Zack are younger than me and, like me are adventurers. They live in Colorado but travel a lot with their mom and dad and get to do amazing things like rock climbing and skiing even though they are just little. Sometimes our shows are just music and dancing, but sometimes we like to mix it up too!

Anna and Mae performing in one of our shows

We were all visiting at my Uncle Marty and Aunt Amrito's in Lake Tahoe. They had two big dogs and we decided to try to train them. I don't remember who had the idea first but all of us cousins thought we would show our progress to the whole family with a dog show. The main event was to show how the dogs could catch and retrieve a ball. The older cousins were the announcers and introduced the dogs and all of us "trainers." I was only three so I probably wasn't as good at it as I thought I was.

Polly training one of the dogs

Here is how it was supposed to work: I was on the deck and the two dogs were on the grass below. The plan was for me to throw the ball, have them catch it and return it to me. I had them lie down while waiting for the ball to be thrown. Every time I was ready to throw the ball, they would stand up, so I would have to go back to the grass and tell them to lie down again. This happened over and over again. Once, I threw the ball backwards, which was not the plan. The other cousins might have helped me out, but everyone was having such a fit of giggles they just let me keep trying. Finally, after several attempts, they caught the ball and brought it back to me. After that one success, we all took a big bow and that ended the training.

From Left to Right: Fiona, Anna, Noah, Zackie, Mae - And of course Me, in the back

Cooking jelly-filled doughnuts for the holidays

CHAPTER TWELVE

THIS SHIP HAS SAILED

My Grams didn't just write down her story, she loves to tell them too. She is very interesting, and hearing about her life reminds me of how lucky I am. Growing up she never imagined she would move to California and be able to travel around the world. At forty-six she went on her first cruise, and now she has been on over fifty. Even though I am only seven, I have been on two! Can you believe it?

One of the best parts about being on a cruise is that once you get there they take care of everything. There is lots of foods and fun activities and shows to watch. Getting ready to go, though, that takes lots of work. We had to get a fancy dress to wear to dinner every night and there were lots of things to learn, like that you never ever call a cruise a boat, it's a ship. Around the time of my first cruise Grandmama and Momma were planning away, and Momma told the other adults, "Well, that ship has sailed." Now, I was pretty young, but I am always listening which is good because the adults in my life need my help, A LOT. So I reminded Momma that the cruise didn't leave until Wednesday, which was still three full days away. Everyone thought it was so funny I remembered when the ship left, even when they didn't. I'm not sure why that was funny but adults are weird sometimes.

Swimming? Reading? So hard to choose.

That time we got to travel around Southwest Alaska. This area is called the panhandle and the traditional people from that area are mostly the Tinglet and Haida Alaskan Natives. Their history brings some of the most recognizable Alaskan cultural art, such as the totem pole. There are many kinds of totem poles. Some totem poles represented a clan and were placed in front of the clans long house, where the family all lived together. Some totem poles represented the life of an important person and were made after their death. Each carving on a totem pole represents a part or character in a story. The original stories are very precious. People pass them down from generation to generation and you can't just go around telling them. In order to tell the story of a totem pole you have to have permission from the artist who carved it.

Luckily, one of our stops was in Hoonah, which is near Juneau, the capital of Alaska. My family lived there for a year before I was born and Momma worked as a tour guide for a summer. Because she was a bear guide she had permission to learn some of their stories and so I was able to hear them from her. I don't have permission to re-tell the stories, but I can say my favorite was about two bears. She also taught me the bear dance. You have to be careful with the bear dance though, because you do it when you want to see a bear. There are three types of bears in Alaska, and while they are all pretty amazing there are times you want to see a bear, and there are times when you really don't. It is important to give the bears their space, especially the big brown bears. That is what they call grizzly bears up in Alaska.

Exploring Ketchikan, not our ship.   *I heart dessert!*

Seeing new places in Alaska, and for me, Hawaii when I got to go on my second cruise, is fun. There are other fun parts to these trips though because there is a lot happening on the ship. My second cruise was special because I got to go with Momma, Grandmama, and Grams – four generations of my women all together. My grandpa Peter was there too, which was great, but he doesn't really count as one of the girls, because well… he's a he. We have a great picture of all of us. My family bought me beautiful Princess dresses to wear to dinner every night. I also had a sparkly princess crown. If I do say so myself, I did look like a princess.

Everyone called me "Princess", maybe because the name of the cruise company was also "Princess". The waiters really spoiled me by getting me my favorite cruise food every night, (alphabet soup) before I even ordered it. The people who kept our room nice also made cool animals out of the towels and left them on my bed for me along with a chocolate treat. Momma let me steal hers too. Ahh, cruising will spoil a girl.

Not only did I get spoiled with nice clothes and good food, I also got a lot of attention because there were not a lot of kids on that big ship. In fact there were only 13 of the over 2,000 passengers. One night we got to go see a magician who asked for a volunteer to help him on the stage. I jumped up and down and yelled "Me, me, me!" He was doing an act which involved balloons. They were in a paper sack, and he asked me what my favorite color was and I told him it was blue. He pulled out a BLACK balloon and made it into an animal. He then asked me my second favorite color, and out came another black balloon, which he made into another animal. He then asked me what my third favorite color was and I answered, with my hands on my hips, "Well, evidently it's going to black because that seems to be the only color you have in your bag". The audience got a big laugh out of that, and he asked me to sit down. I think he did that because I was taking over his act.

There are really too many awesome memories from my cruising days. Adventuring in Alaska, exploring beautiful Hawaii, and all of the great people and things on the actual cruise. I hope your parents will take you on one some day, or if you have to, wait until you are grown up and take yourself!

It's all about accessorizing.

*When you get dressed up,
you just got to pose.*

CHAPTER THIRTEEN
MY SEVENTH BIRTHDAY

As I get older, my mom always makes sure we mark my Birthday with something really special. It is because when she was a little girl her family moved just before her fourth birthday. Since they were in a new location, they didn't know many people and she had a bad birthday party, so now she is obsessed with making my birthdays spectacular.

Once, for my Snow White themed birthday, she and Grandmama made a cake showing Snow White on a hill above the dwarves' mine. Not only was it huge, the mine had little twinkle lights INSIDE that sparkled like diamonds. For my seventh birthday, I actually asked to skip my regular birthday party. Not wanting a party may seem like a strange thing for me to do, but there was a very good reason. My Aunt and Uncle and my cousins, Anna and Mae, had just moved to Texas. This meant I missed seeing them on my summer trip to the lower forty-eight before they moved. I really missed them and I wanted to see their new house. So I asked if we could go to Texas for my birthday. I couldn't believe it when Momma actually said okay. She even said I could have a party at the American Girl doll store.

I have two American Girl dolls. They came as the characters of Victorian Samantha and pioneer Kristen – but I renamed them Andrea and Pip because I love being original. The party was held in their special Birthday Room. It was so beautiful! I got to sit on a pink throne. Everything was pink. I actually prefer blue, but I understand sometimes being a princess, in a princess room, calls for a lot of pink and a lot of sparkle. I even got to wear a pink crown. My cousin's got crowns too. Not only were my cousins Anna and Mae and their mom at the party, Grams came from California too. Of course Momma and Grandmama were there, but the boys, Uncle Joel and Grandpa Peter, stayed home. Too much glitter. Uncle Joel calls it "devil's dust" and says it is forbidden in his house because it sticks to everything. He is a middle school teacher and doesn't like it when his students ask why he has sparkles.

Grandpa Peter might have actually enjoyed a good tea party, but he doesn't have the hair to pull off a crown, and he didn't have an American Girl doll to bring along. Oh yes, we all had an American Girl doll, even the grownups, and there were special chairs for all the dolls so they could sit at the table with us.

We did some fun things before lunch, which, by the way, was delicious, and then a beautiful birthday cake. It was a really special day that I will never forget. After the party, we all shopped at the store and my cousins got me a birthday present. Some ear muffs for Pip. It was a great gift because I am always wearing earmuffs. I don't know why but they make me feel better so I wear them all the time, even in hot places like Mexico in the summer. What a fun day!

Mama and Grandmama purchased gift items for me to enjoy when I play with my American Dolls.

For my eighth birthday, I'm wondering what surprises Momma will come up with. I do know it's going to be epic, like all my adventures.

CHAPTER FOURTEEN
WHAT THE FUTURE HOLDS

I've come a long way in my short life. From a five pound baby into a toddler who loved to build things with cans of vegetables, with my dolls in their buggy, and sitting in weird things like frying pans and drawers. Then there were the preschool years. Other memories I have when I was much younger was doing regular learning things like coloring and painting, helping mom cook and helping the other kids with "works" I was good at. My preschool, like all Montessori call our learning times "works."

Now my work includes regular chores and helping Grandmama keep her classroom clean along with being a third grade student. Sometimes being a kid seems like I am forever waiting, but sometimes it also seems like time is just flying by. Of course those times are always when I am having the most fun and I can't stand for it to end.

So this is my life so far. There has been a lot of challenges that have helped make me Alaskan Tuf. There has also been so much good stuff to make it all worth it. I hope you have enjoyed my story. Who knows - - I may write the next "chapter." Eight to Teenager? Momma tells me the teen years will be "interesting." A story in the future! If this is enjoyed by anyone who reads it as much as I hope it will, remember to tell your own stories. You can write it down like me, or just around the dinner table or when making a new friend. Be happy, have fun, do exciting things and dare to dream. Until next time, your best friend from Alaska - - Pollyanna.

Summer

Fall

Winter

Spring

A THOUSAND WORDS: THE PHOTO GALLERY

The extra hours of sun in the summer help us grow some GIANT vegetables.

Me and Grams, who helped me write this book, doing one of my favorite things – reading..

Planting our herb garden. Grandmama invented a pully system to raise the pallet up and keep it safe from the moose.

You can never be too safe with UV rays

Sometimes outdoor storage doesn't quite work in Alaskan winters. This WAS a snowglobe.

The famous light up cake of my 6th Birthday

A THOUSAND WORDS: THE PHOTO GALLERY CONTINUED

The foam hook doesn't catch many fish, but it is the safest way to learn how to cast.

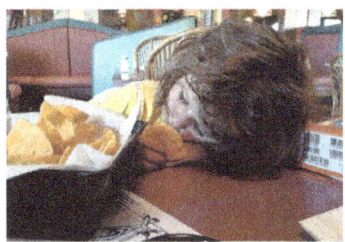

Fishing is fun, but also exhausting. We took a break from dipnetting and went out to dinner, but I passed out before I could even get this chip to my mouth!

A girl has got to keep up on her current events – Just kidding, I'm totally reading the comics.

Dance leotards and muck boots, the true Alaskan spring wardrobe.

We walk Moka everyday, then the kittens decided to follow along. Now they walk with us all the time – I think they like going for a walk even more than the dog!

No long TSA lines at this airport.

Waiting for my sleigh ride.

Ready for my plane trip to the Mainland.

This is a wonderful, biographical story for children that is very relatable. Its sly humor makes it enjoyable for adults as well. With lovely photos taken from the life of the real Pollyanna, and written from the point of view of a precocious seven-year old, it offers delightful glimpses into her life.

Shanti Amrito

I loved it! It's in the style of a reality show and fish-out-of-water interpretation of life in Alaska, by a very intelligent and funny seven-year old. You will return to childhood as you see Alaska through the eyes of a unique child with with a fascinating viewpoint.

Martin Richard

Children will love reading this book to imagine what life in Alaska would be like for a young child. They will be inspired by Polly's zest for adventure.

Peter Roys

www.ingramcontent.com/pod-product-compliance
Lightning Source LLC
Chambersburg PA
CBHW061105070526
44579CB00011B/137